Ask
About
Animals

Acknowledgments

Executive Editor: Diane Sharpe
Supervising Editor: Stephanie Muller
Design Manager: Sharon Golden
Page Design: Simon Balley Design Associates
Photography: Heather Angel: page 7; Bruce Coleman: pages 11, 23, 30; NHPA: page 27; Natural Science Photo Library: cover (top right); Oxford Scientific Films: cover (middle right), pages 15, 19; Tony Stone: cover (bottom right).

Library of Congress Cataloging-in-Publication Data

Lawrie, Christine.
    Ask about animals/Christine Lawrie; illustrated by Maggie Downer.
      p.   cm. — (Read all about it)
    Includes index.
    ISBN 0-8114-5729-X Hardcover
    ISBN 0-8114-3709-4 Softcover
    1. Animals — Miscellanea — Juvenile literature.   [1. Animals — Miscellanea.]   I. Downer, Maggie, ill.
II. Title.   III. Series: Read all about it (Austin, Tex.)
QL49.L3485   1995
591—dc20

94-28180
CIP
AC

4 5 6 7 8 9 00 PO 00 99

Ask
About
Animals

Christine Lawrie

Illustrated by
Maggie Downer

STECK-VAUGHN
C O M P A N Y
ELEMENTARY • SECONDARY • ADULT • LIBRARY

I love animals.

I'll ask you questions about some animals. See if you can guess their names.

What very small insect has a bright
red shell with black spots? It lives
in the garden.

Turn the page to find the answer.

It's a ladybug!

The ladybug's shell covers its wings.

Gardeners like ladybugs.
Ladybugs eat insects that can
harm garden plants.

Let's pretend we are on the plains of Africa.

What huge animal has big ears
and a trunk? It has tusks made
of ivory.

Turn the page to find the answer.

9

It's an elephant!

Elephants are the biggest animals that live on land.

10

Elephants use their trunks to pick up food and to suck up water. They squirt the water into their mouths.

Now let's pretend we are in the desert of Saudi Arabia.

What animal has a long neck
and a hump on its back?
It can go for a long time
without water.

Turn the page to find the answer.

It's a camel!

People use camels to carry them across the desert.

Camels can live in very hot, dry places. The fat they store in their humps can be turned into water.

15

Let's pretend we are in
Australia.

What animal has a long tail, big back legs, and moves by jumping? It carries its baby in a pouch.

Turn the page to find the answer.

It's a kangaroo!

Kangaroos can jump very fast.

A baby kangaroo is called a joey.

Let's pretend we are near the
North Pole.

20

What animal is very big and
has white fur? It hunts seals
and fish.

Turn the page to find the answer.

It's a polar bear!

Polar bears are very good
swimmers.

Polar bear cubs are born during
the winter in a den under the snow.
In the spring, they go hunting with
their mother.

Let's pretend we are in a
rain forest in Brazil.

What animal slithers through the leaves and branches? It is very long and has no legs.

Turn the page to find the answer.

This snake is a boa constrictor.
It lives in the rain forest of Brazil.

Boa constrictors squeeze their
prey to death. Then they swallow
it whole.

Let's guess one more animal
that might be in the garden.

28

What has eight legs and spins
a web to catch its food?

It eats flies and other insects
that get stuck in its web.

Turn the page to find the answer.

It's a spider!

You guessed all the animals!

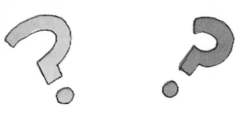

Can you remember all the animals that are in this book?

Index